MYTH MEN ™

GUARDIANS OF THE LEGEND

PERSEUS

THE BOY WITH SUPER POWERS

BY LAURA GERINGER

ILLUSTRATED BY PETER BOLLINGER

SCHOLASTIC INC.

NEW YORK TORONTO LONDON AUCKLAND SYDNEY

For my heroic Adam and his kung fu brother. — L. G.   *For my family.* — P. B.

Text copyright © 1996 by Laura Geringer. • Illust.. ger.
MYTH MEN is a trademark of Laura Geringer a............................
Published by Scholastic Inc. • Book design b...

12 11 10 9 8 7 6 5 4 3 2 1   6 7 8 9/9 0 1/0
Printed in the U.S.A.   08
First Scholastic printing, November 1996

PERSEUS BECAME A famous hero when he was only a boy, too young to grow a beard and just old enough to have his first adventure.

His father was Zeus, king of the gods. His mother, Danae, was a sweet and beautiful princess locked up in a dark dungeon by her mad father, King Acrisius, who could not bear the thought of his daughter marrying.

One night, while Danae wept and watched the sky, listening to the dismal howl of the guard dogs circling her prison cell, a shower of light came toward her, so bright she had to close her eyes.

When she opened them, a giant golden man stood before her, and in his hand he held a bolt of lightning.

"Don't be afraid," he pleaded. "I love you."

But Danae was not afraid. She was delighted. "Will you visit me every night?" she asked.

Zeus knew he could not promise to visit Danae every night, for he was a very busy god. So he made another promise. "I will make our son a hero," he said.

And that very night, Perseus was born.

PERSEUS WAS NOT a big baby. But when he was hungry, he wailed loudly. One dark night, crazy King Acrisius heard that wail and hurried out to consult a fortune-teller for advice.

And the king went home, muttering to himself.

The next morning, determined to trick the fates, crazy King Acrisius put Danae and the baby Perseus in a wooden chest without food or water and sent them out to sea.

Poor Perseus. Poor Danae. They bobbed about on the waves for days. But Zeus kept the winds gentle and guided them safely through rocks and reefs. Finally, the chest got caught in the strong net of a fisherman named Dictys. Imagine the good man's surprise when he opened the chest!

Now, the island Perseus and his mother had landed upon was ruled by an evil king named Polydectes, one of the worst villains in the world. When King Polydectes saw the beautiful Danae, he wanted to marry her. Of course she said no. So, biding his time, he invited her to live in his palace.

As the years passed, Perseus grew taller, stronger, and more handsome than any young man on the island. He was the best at running races and fighting.

But he was not happy.

"You have no father," teased the other boys. And they did not let Perseus into their games. When he explained that his father was Zeus, king of the gods, they dared him to prove it.

Night after night, Perseus would listen to his mother's tales of heroes, and of those times when gods appeared to mortals on earth and guided them on their quests. He wished his father Zeus would come and tell him how to begin his life as a hero. He dreamed sometimes of a boy who could fly, a boy who could go anywhere and do anything, a boy with super powers!

"Perseus," said King Polydectes one morning, "isn't it time you went out into the world?"

"I pray to be given a task by the gods," Perseus replied.

"Let me see," said the king, rubbing his chin thoughtfully. "What, in your opinion, is the most terrible monster in all of Greece?"

"Medusa," said Perseus with no hesitation, for he had often heard the story of the ugliest of the three ugly Gorgon Sisters — so hideous that anyone who dared look at her was turned to stone.

YOUR PRAYERS HAVE BEEN ANSWERED. THE GODS HAVE CHOSEN TO SPEAK THROUGH *ME*. HERE IS YOUR MISSION. BRING ME BACK THE HEAD OF MEDUSA — OR LOSE YOUR *OWN*.

 SO PERSEUS SAID good-bye to his mother and to his friend, the good fisherman Dictys. And he went forth to kill Medusa.

But he had no idea where to find her.

"Zeus!" Perseus prayed, as he had prayed many times before. "If you are truly my father, show me a sign."

And to his amazement, this time the clouds parted. A shaft of light shone down, and along that white path in the sky walked a young man in winged shoes and a winged hat who waved at Perseus, greeting him like an old friend. It was Hermes, messenger of the gods!

AND HAVE YOU HEARD, INSTEAD OF HAIR SHE HAS POISONOUS *SNAKES* GROWING OUT OF HER HEAD?

I'VE HEARD.

INSTEAD OF TEETH, SHE HAS *DEADLY FANGS*. HER BODY — *UGH!* — IS COVERED ALL OVER WITH IRON SCALES. HER CLAWS ARE AS SHARP AS RAZORS. AND HER ENORMOUS WINGS...

DID MY FATHER SEND YOU TO HELP ME?

HE'S MY FATHER *TOO*, YOU KNOW. AND YES, HE DID SEND ME. TOO BUSY TO COME *HIMSELF*, OF COURSE. HERE — THIS IS YOURS! YOUR FIRST JOB IS TO SHINE IT SO THAT IT GLOWS LIKE A STAR.

And he handed Perseus a beautiful shield.

Perseus thought this an odd way to start an adventure, but his heart filled with joy. With Hermes by his side, anything seemed possible! So he did as he was told, polishing away until he could see his own face in the shield as clearly as in a mirror.

GOOD, NOW FOR YOUR SWORD!

And taking off his own gleaming weapon, curved like a sickle, Hermes handed it to Perseus, who stuck it proudly in his belt.

Hermes rose like a seagull into the air, higher and higher. "Here are *your* wings!" he said, laughing. And he threw Perseus a pair of winged shoes like his own.

QUICKLY, BROTHER! PUT THESE ON AND LET'S FLY. SOON IT WILL BE TOO DARK TO FIND THE GRAY SISTERS. *STEADY NOW!*

Perseus rose up, orbiting Hermes like a bat gone wild. Suddenly he felt swift as an eagle, light as a leaf on the wind, carefree as the boy he used to dream about, the boy who could go anywhere and do anything — the boy with super powers!

And he took off toward the setting sun with his brother close behind.

4

P ERSEUS FLEW OVER mountains and valleys, over farms and fields of wheat, over tiny towns and big cities, over roads and rivers and silvery groves of olive trees, and finally over a vast salt plain, icy white, where the wind was fierce.

"Why do we need the Gray Sisters?" he complained. "Why can't we just go straight to Medusa?"

"Hush," said Hermes sternly, "keep a sharp lookout, Perseus. The Gray Sisters come only in twilight and never by the light of sun or moon. Watch closely now or you'll miss them. I think I hear their voices."

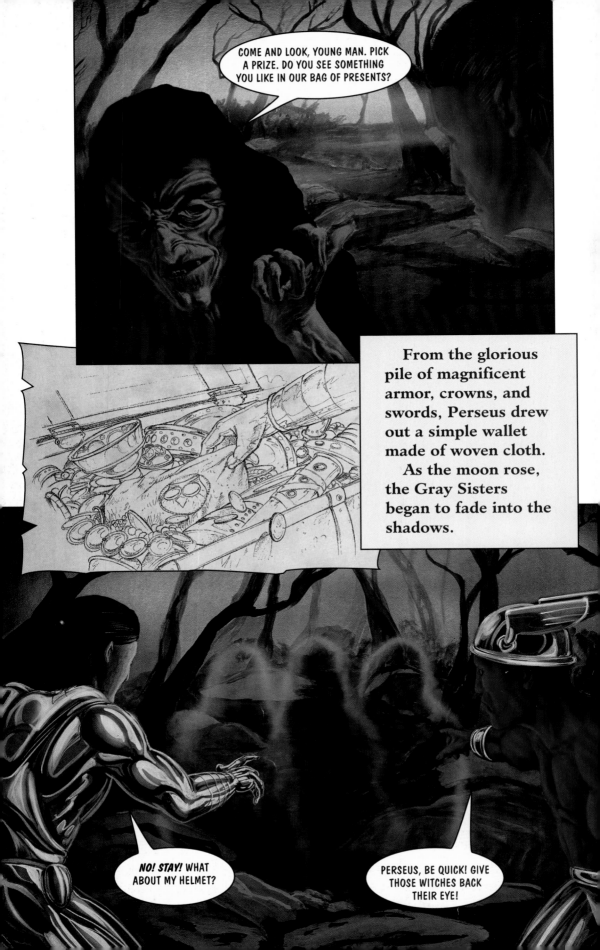

The moon, gigantic now, had all but erased the Gray Sisters. Perseus ran up to one of the sisters and clapped the eye back into the place he guessed it would go, for he could no longer see her face.

Cackling, she plucked a helmet from the dark night air and slammed it on his head before she disappeared altogether.

As soon as the helmet was on his head, an amazing thing happened to Perseus! He disappeared too! One moment he stood there, a good-looking young man with a sickle-shaped sword in his belt and a shield shining as brightly as any star. And the next, he was gone without a trace!

5

PERSEUS WAS INVISIBLE — even to Hermes! With his brother by his side, Perseus flew high over the ocean — so high he could barely hear the silver surf crashing against the cliffs. A meteor flashed across the sky. By its fiery light, Perseus could see what looked like a graveyard in the sand. As he drew closer, he could tell that the stones were not graves but hundreds of people, all turned to stone. There was a stone soldier, a stone woman, her hands raised to the sky as if begging the gods to bring her back to life, and a stone king, riding in his chariot. But saddest of all was a boy, marching proudly off to war. He looked so full of courage, but he was stone, all stone.

A dark cloud passed over Perseus when he saw that boy. He felt he was looking at himself turned to stone.

COURAGE, PERSEUS! MEDUSA IS FAST ASLEEP BEHIND THOSE BLACK BOULDERS JUST AHEAD. WHEN HER HIDEOUS FACE APPEARS IN YOUR SHIELD, DON'T LOOK AWAY. REMEMBER, HER *REFLECTION* CANNOT KILL YOU.

WHO IS THIS BOY? I FEEL I KNOW HIM SOMEHOW.

"His name was Bellerophon," said Hermes. "If you do your part, he may live again and become a hero some day!"

Inching forward, Perseus now saw the three awful Gorgon Sisters in an ugly knot. As they dozed, the snakes on their heads stood straight up and rattled. And their steely scales glistened as they rubbed their wings together like gigantic insects.

Suddenly, there was Medusa, coming straight toward him. Roaring and gnashing her fangs, her savage face filled his shield. Perseus stepped closer and, still looking into the mirror shield, raised his sword high.

"Now!" cried Hermes. "Strike, Perseus! You have only one chance!"

Twisting and coiling, Medusa's snaky locks dripped venom and filled him with horror.

But most horrible of all were her eyes!

6

THE HEROES' STROKE fell like a flash of lightning, sharp and true. And the head of Medusa rolled.

But Medusa's head was still alive!

Quickly, Perseus snatched that trophy, snakes and all, and stuffed it safely inside his magic wallet, where it continued to hiss!

The two immortal Gorgon Sisters awoke with a roar and stared around wildly, looking for someone to turn to stone. Perseus closed his eyes and soared up, up, up in his winged shoes, high over the headless Medusa.

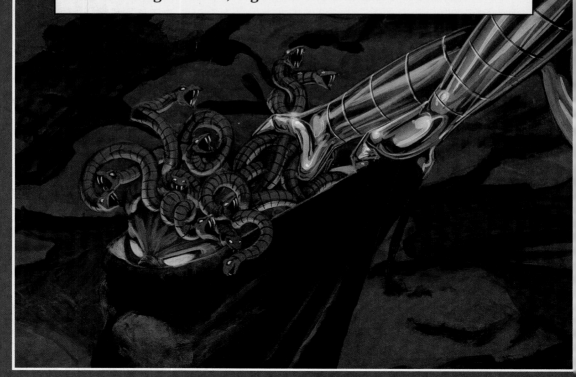

Then a miracle happened. As Perseus flew over Medusa's graveyard, several drops of the monster's blood fell from his wallet onto the stone boy Bellerophon — and the boy came back to life!

At the same moment, out of Medusa's neck flew a glorious white winged horse. Swift and graceful, it was as beautiful as Medusa was hideous, and it brightened the heavens around its place of birth with beams of light!

"Pegasus!" Bellerophon called, as if he had known the majestic white horse all his life. And Pegasus came to him. The boy mounted Pegasus and sailed in wide arcs from cloud to cloud.

"No," answered Perseus. "But I bring a promise from the gods. Someday, you will grow up to be a hero."

"I wish I could see your face. Thank you for saving my life and for freeing my people from Medusa!"

And Bellerophon flew off into the clouds on the broad back of the beautiful white winged horse, with the two immortal Gorgons clashing and roaring below, their rasping voices almost drowned by the angry sea.

Perseus swelled with pride. He hoped his father Zeus was listening. He looked into his shield. His face looked older than it had before he killed Medusa. At last, he was a hero!

"You'll need Medusa's head for your next adventure, Perseus," said a gentle voice by his shoulder. It was Hermes. "When you're home and safe at last, call me and I'll come. Don't be surprised when you return — time passes quickly in the land of the Gray Sisters. Good-bye, brother. Good-bye!"

"Wait!" Perseus yelled after him. "I'll miss you, Hermes. And, by the way, what *is* my next adventure?" But his brother had already dropped out of sight, and Perseus did not have to wait long to find out.

His next adventure was just around the corner — but that's another story entirely.